POETRY SONGBOOK

Write your way to happiness

DEVELOP A LOVE OF POETRY, WORDS AND IMAGINATION, FOR ULTIMATE HAPPINESS, HEALTH AND CONFIDENCE

JENNIFER MARY JONES

*With love & light
Jennifer
xxx*

authors
AND CO.

CONTENTS

ABOUT THE AUTHOR

Jennifer Mary Jones is a lifelong poet, a spoken word artist, singer, yoga coach, and dedicated military wife. Jennifer grew up on the idyllic Isle of Man, in the British Isles, surrounded by nature and the sea, raised by her Scottish mother and English father. Jen lives a happy life with her husband William, and their dog Wilma.

Poetry Songbook gracefully and refreshingly explores the life phases of the human condition. This book is a beautiful poetry journal for the reader to literally experience becoming a writer, by journeying along, creating their own collection of poetry, writing as they read.

Jennifer brings us poems written across three decades from her childhood, adolescence, and early adulthood. This is a celebration of Jennifer's life's musings, daydreams, precious memories, and poetic songs from her heart.

There is journal space alongside the poems for real interactive creativity for the reader to enjoy along the way. What makes this book an original gem is that it presents the poems along with comments from the author telling us the context and inspiration behind the poems, as well as some excellent 'Poet Prompts' to spark the reader's imagination.

Jennifer completed a BA Hons. English Language & Sociolinguistics Degree at Lancaster University in England, and Carleton University in Canada. Followed by a Master's Degree in Publishing & Language, at the Oxford International Centre for Publishing. She enjoys performing her work through spoken word and song. This is Jennifer's debut written poetry publication.

 instagram.com/poetrysongbook

For my Mum & Dad
I love you
Thank you

WELCOME

a beautiful welcome to you.

I am Jennifer Mary, named after my dad's favourite schoolteacher, and my darling grandma Mary.

This book is my story through poetry, written over the last thirty years, and I am beyond excited to share it with you. As well as sharing my poetry, I have included some thought-provoking 'Poet Prompts' for you to try out in the gorgeous journal space alongside each poem, so you can fall in love with poetry, words, and your imagination.

Whether you are an experienced writer or just starting out, this book is a great and original way to help you to enjoy your writing. It will help you to connect with your imagination, to feel creative, and to dramatically boost your happiness, improve your overall wellbeing and supercharge your confidence.

Writing poetry is part of my DNA. Since I was a young child, I've loved to play with words and experiment with the creative use of language to convey a message of emotion. I am fascinated with clever metaphors in day-to-day language, like workplace conversations, sports commentary, and advertising. It is mesmerising to witness the power that words convey in our global politics and international relations, as well as closer to home, during the epic life-changing promises made at marriage ceremonies. Words are powerful.

This journal will naturally encourage you to reflect and think about your own personal life experiences. As you read and write along with the pages, you can watch as, like magic, your personal life experiences begin to take form as poetry. This is both a writing experience and a soothing human experience too, as you journey from your childhood through the years, using your adventures to fill the pages.

When I was a child, my lovely dad, Alan, sat with me and read every page of each book of the *Chronicles of Narnia*, by C.S. Lewis. My dad is a busy, hard-working man, so his bedtime stories remain treasured moments of my life. My mum, Anne, instilled a deep love of books within me from day one. Mum always told me that 'books are precious'. My most memorable times reading with Mum were when we read the wonderful *Anne of Green Gables* and its sequels, by Lucy Maud Montgomery. Mum and I would take turns reading the pages and I remember us laughing, beaming, and crying together as we journeyed through Green Gables.

Do you remember your school days well? As a schoolgirl, I had a great imagination and confidence, often having my classmates laughing their heads off when I put forward another wacky idea. Notably, my schoolmates recall a moment I questioned what it would be like to 'actually be' a big girl's blouse... I was also academic and studious and immensely proud when, in sixth form, I was appointed as the school's Chief Librarian!

At university, I really found my tribe while studying Linguistics and English Language. Sociolinguistics became a real passion subject matter - the look of words, the structure of sentences, and the huge variety of sounds the words can make when spoken aloud in varied accents and dialects, is fascinating to me. Looking back, when given a choice of extra subject modules, I always selected the juicy creative stylistics modules and took any opportunity to read, analyse or write poetry.

My second year was spent abroad at Carleton University in Ottawa. Like one of my heroes, Anne of Green Gables, I was now living my best life in Canada! The year in Ottawa was life-changing. It shaped me so much and gave me so many of my life values that still stand so true today. I met treasured friends who I still see regularly, nearly two decades on.

Living in Canada, I witnessed four clearly defined seasons for the first time. I've always been fascinated by the changing seasons and the ageing of each year - the turning, the growing, the wisdom, the repeat. Life to me is full of beauty - beauty in kindness, community, and goodwill, as well as beauty in nature and wildlife. I love to reference nature in my writing. It is like taking a photograph of a gorgeous scene, though using words on a page instead of an image in ink.

My Canadian adventure began with a bright, colourful autumn, which shrivelled and hardened into a silver-white winter of icicles and ice skating on the historic Rideau Canal. Winter saw temperatures of minus 40 degrees when I would snatch a thrill of fresh air after varsity swimming team practice and see the ends of my hair literally turn to ice before my eyes. The winter melted into a pretty springtime and ultimately, a sunshine-filled summer. It was a magical year. I turned twenty during these months and I felt a real coming of age.

As a person, I have always been caring and super connected to my own and other people's emotions. Although I may not always show these emotions outwardly, I feel them greatly inside. When I see pain in the world, I feel it physically. I am over-empathetic. I'm hypersensitive. I care deeply. I am kind. I do not tolerate bullying. When I witness bullying indirectly around me or directly towards me, I always feel deep sadness on behalf of the bully and I, perhaps foolishly, try to help them to feel better with kind encouragement or generosity. It doesn't always end in success, however, it feels right to me to shine light and love where there is darkness, sadness, or suffering.

As someone who puts others' happiness ahead of my own, I historically struggled to stand up for what I want. As a result of attempting to change this passive stance, I have worked hard to express myself and my wishes as an adult. Poetry has helped me to do this. Becoming more confident and more expressive of our needs and wishes, and appearing to change, sometimes means others may no longer know how to take us. As a result of becoming more confident and able to express myself, I have sadly lost some important relationships with both friends and family members. I am, of course, saddened by this loss and I send them so much love and light, however, it feels game-changing to have found an authentic, honest voice of my own.

It is in the dark moments that we can truly learn to dance in our own light. I urge you to use your emotions to superpower what you write. Through writing you can tackle tough memories, honour hardships you have faced, and channel those dig-deep moments that you have experienced in your lifetime. To make your writing soulful, turn to losses, reflect on crossroad moments, and remember to search for your sense of belonging. Likewise, turn to memories and moments of ecstasy and uttermost joy to flick pure gold onto your pages.

My poetry explores the human condition. I believe that my life experiences and personality naturally help me feel deep emotions, which is a wonderful way to tune in and evoke feeling to let poetry come onto a page. I write mostly on themes of love and loss. I, like so many, have loved and lost. I have felt for much of my life, simultaneously in both love and in loss. I'm a Libra star sign and I love, love, love to feel balanced and to feel in love - in love with my husband, with my friendships, with the dog, with my clothes, with words, with my purpose, with my holidays, with my work, with my whole lifestyle! Love lights me up and makes me feel safe and perfect. In love, I am exactly where I am supposed to be. I highly recommend this way of life. Let yourself shine with love and feel deeply happy and share this beautiful happiness with others, as you spend time with them and go about your days.

Sadness, when present, consumes my every cell, my whole being. As such, I don't like to sit in sadness for long. I know it is important to grieve and let go, so, over the years I have turned to writing to release sorrow. I also use singing and swimming in the same way - to let go, to release, and to reset my nervous system.

My first memorable experience of deep trauma was when a very close friend of mine died very suddenly and unexpectedly in 2010. She remains one of the best humans I've ever met. She and I laughed together so much. We were inseparable at university. She will always be within me in my memories, and I'll always talk about her brilliance. I will always be in awe of her light. She will always be just twenty-four years old.

I remember the moment when I first saw the words;

 'grief is the price we pay for love'

— QUEEN ELIZABETH II

This balance rings true to me in so many ways, from deepest love and loss in friendships to losing family by death or, perhaps more sadly, by misunderstanding. Love and loss go hand in hand. They say people come into our lives for reasons and seasons. They may shine on us like the sun, or they might dampen and darken our days. The important things I have learnt are to make sure you can bring yourself back into balance, act with kindness, learn from experiences, and stay on your own true north.

I find words comforting – the reading, the listening, and the writing of words keep me grounded. They help me stay on my true north, and weather any storm.

As you read the next pages, I invite you to explore your own human condition. Let yourself journey down memory lane, revel in nostalgia, remember something long lost, or simply feel love, remember how much love is inside of you and how much you are deeply loved. You are a beautiful person, inside and out. Remember, you are someone's hero, and you are doing a brilliant job. You are here, now, for a reason, and you are so very important.

Poetry Songbook captures poetry and song from within me, deep in my soul. It has been crafted to help you connect with, find, and create your very own Songbook. This book is structured to take you on a sweet tour of my poems, through my childhood, teens, twenties, and thirties, precisely so you can reminisce or ponder on these beautiful stages of your own life. The whole book is full of treats to help you unlock your imagination and write your own poetry and song along the way... to write your way to happiness…

Poet Prompt:

This is your very first 'Poet Prompt'… I encourage you to write with a real pen and paper, as this makes your writing experience much more mindful and calming than typing on a computer, tablet or mobile phone. Grab that pen or pencil! Fill up these pages… they are yours.

I hope you enjoy this gorgeous journey into poetry. My wish is that it will spark creative thinking within you, my new friend. I hope you take comfort in my work. I wish you and your people happiness, health, confidence in abundance, lightness of heart, and most of all, love.

With my love

Jennifer Mary x

MY CREATIVE PROCESS

*W*hen I feel a poem coming on, I grab a pen (or even my mobile phone if I am on the move) and scribble it down. It typically comes as one flow. All the words, one after the other. I feel completely calm, pure and full of light when the words fly in. It feels like I already know the poem, as if it is a song from within. It feels like a surge of emotion comes into my heart, my imagination fires up, words come through my mind, and I quickly get the words onto paper before the words have gone from my mind.

I have always written in this way. I recall, as a child, rushing to find a pencil and paper to write down a poem or story. Latterly, I have sat down to write and been able to relax into the zone to let poems come in, sometimes one after another. Sometimes I've been walking down the street when my best work has come to mind. *Solidarity from the Sky* came to me in this way. This is one of my very favourite and more treasured poems, written on an autumn day in 2020, when I found out that my husband had just parachuted into the Ukraine with the British Army.

There is no right or wrong method to write. There are so many ways. If your writing style is different to mine, then that's great. It is so nice to all be different and able to inspire and support one another. Through differences, we can come together, learn from one another and have great creative conversations.

Remember that a poem is a simple song from a heart. It is truth. It can be read introvertedly, or spoken, or sung aloud extrovertedly to the world. Scholars may define a poem in a more precise way, but I believe that a poem can be three words long, or three pages long! It certainly does not have to rhyme. It is whatever your heart wants to sing.

If you deeply wish to write, yet you aren't sure where to begin with your own poetry, I encourage you to try out the Poets Prompts throughout this book, using the journal space and you will soon learn to connect with your own songs within your soul. I hope you love every moment.

YOUR CREATIVE PROCESS

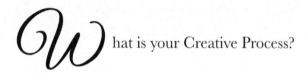hat is your Creative Process?

Poet Prompt:

Have a think about your happy writing place…

Where is your best place to write?

What time of day do you prefer to write?

Do you have a favourite writing accompaniment or companion?

POEMS OF MY CHILDHOOD

I was a very sweet and fun-loving child. Growing up in a busy, active household in the 1990s left me little time to myself in my youngest years. I was always with someone, or lots of people, surrounded by other children, or grandparents, or my parents and siblings, the fish, guinea pigs, cats, and the dog! The house was active. It was non-stop. I recall the sounds of play, of my mum baking in the kitchen, distant sports commentary on the television, and piano music all swirled into one.

Naturally full of creativity and energy, I really did mean well, although I was often told to stop speaking, or not to speak at all, to wait my turn, or to temper my exuberance. Quietly, I would write stories, poems, read books, draw, make paper dolls, create newsletters for make-believe clubs, make up shows to perform when we had visitors, and, of course, play with my epic 1990s post office set! It was within this quiet that I could feel the magic and joy of my imagination coming alive.

These were great years.

There is real simplicity within the next poems. They are examples of my first attempts to write poetry - something I would take pride in and want to share with my parents and teachers, for their feedback and encouragement.

Before reading the next poems, try out this childhood meditation to get yourself connected to your own inner child.

CHILDHOOD MEDITATION

*T*his meditation is a wonderful experience you can come back to time and time again.

1. Pay attention to your breathing. Enjoy the breath entering, flowing about and leaving your body, a repeated circle of life.

2. Think back to a time when you were a little child. Imagine yourself vividly.

> *What are you doing?*
> *What clothes and shoes are you wearing?*
> *Where are you?*
> *Who is with you?*
> *Is there a favourite toy nearby?*

3. Now imagine someone, a kind, familiar person, saying something to you, something very special, that

you need to hear. Listen… keep listening until you hear that special message for your inner child.

4. Now, close your eyes and place your hands on your heart.

5. Repeat the message to yourself three times. Breathing in through the nose and out through your mouth, sighing to release and inhaling to heal and enclose the happiness this brings.

YOUR CHILDHOOD

*P*oet Prompt:

What did your meditation bring up?

Write down three words to represent your childhood.

Jot down any memories and learnings here…

THE WORLD OF MAGIC

The world of magic!
The magician waves his wand,
A rabbit appears.

The world of magic!
People disappear. Goodness.
Magic is in the air.

The world of magic!
A beautiful assistant,
Waiting for her part.

The world of magic
Is a very scary place.
Lions, knives, swords.

The world of magic
Is not to be tinkered with.
Bad things might happen.

This one was from way back at primary school. It is so sweet reading it and recalling my imagination as a child.

Poet Prompt:

Take yourself on a playful day out. Go to somewhere that your inner child dreams to go - a trampoline park, a theme park, a round of crazy golf, a day at the beach building sand-castles, or even a day at the circus! The more playful, the better.

WALKING HOME IN THE DARK

A spooky walk all the way,
It is always quiet and black.
There is only a lamp in the third window,
All the rest is silent.

I tiptoe through the land of ghosts and ghouls
And other scary things,
Like boogie men and cannibals
And spirits of great kings…

It's a long walk home,
Especially at night.

This one was a competition winner! In primary school, aged nine, I wrote this at school. It was selected by my teacher and entered for a competition called 'Over the Moon'. I was absolutely thrilled when it was published along with the other winning poems. I was so proud to see my work inside a real book.

Poet Prompt:

Write a little poem about something you find challenging. Think of that fear head-on and use your words to magic it away.

Bonus Poet Prompt!

When you have written a poem that you really love, why not enter one of your poems into a competition? There are so many poetry competitions from local ones to worldwide ones. What do you have to lose? You could even host a poetry competition to raise funds for a special charity.

THE DAY BEFORE EASTER

Every year, young lambs appear.
All around the silvery meadows lie daffodils.
Sweet little chicks pop out of their shells.
Tomorrow will be Easter day!
Everyone come and sing with us.
Remember the true reason for Easter.

BONFIRE

Bonfires burning, smoke in the air.
Over Britain, they are everywhere.
Night has come, it's getting dark.
Fire is out in the park.
In the garden, ash is flying.
Remember this night,
Every year we celebrate.

AUTUMN

Autumn time, leaves are falling.
Under leaves lie little creatures,
Telling secrets of the spring.
Up above birds hide their heads under their wings.
Many children like to kick the leaves.
No more leaves will fall today.

These little sequences are snippets of my very early poetry. I was around ten years old. As you can see, they are all acrostic poems, spelling out a keyword vertically downwards.

Poet Prompt:

What is your favourite season? Write and sketch about it and see what flows. Choose a favourite word from your notes and make a little acrostic to reveal the word vertically downwards at the left-hand side of the poem. These also make lovely thoughtful tokens to include in a birthday or greeting card, using your friend's name as the acrostic.

SILENCE IS GOLDEN

Silence — voices freeze, nobody speaks.
Afraid, lonely, thinking deeply.
Awkward moments,
Wondering what to say.
Trying not to upset a close friend.
Feeling lost and distressed.
Upsetting moments, deep thoughts.
Should you? Should you not?
Why did you? What for?
Respecting others, too shocked to speak…
You don't believe you have been chosen.
Think of the special times,
The fun that was shared.
The thought that comes to mind is,
Silence is golden.

Ahh, school days! This poem was what I wrote down when my school class was told off by a rather disgruntled teacher after we made what she deemed too much noise! We were told to stay in silence for the remainder of the lesson and to write a poem about why silence is golden. I was twelve years old. Reflecting on this 'punishment' as an adult, I find it insightful. However, I did earn a merit stamp for my efforts!

Poet Prompt:

Think back to your school days and write about one of your clearest memories.

POEMS OF MY TEENAGE YEARS

I went from being a highly organised young scholar, and one of the tallest in my primary school class, to becoming one of the most petite and happy-go-lucky kids in my high school year. During my first year of high school, I was bullied for 'being ugly', having 'bad shoes' and for wearing glasses. My lovely mum would discretely remove blue fountain pen ink flick stains from the back of my school blouse each week for many months. Kids are naturally so blunt and can say and do some very unkind things. However, overall, I didn't let it bother me too deeply. I believe it was thanks to my imagination that I remained a happy, joyful and content teenager.

This is totally a Hollywood cliché, but at age fourteen I literally blossomed overnight. With contact lenses I was unstoppable!

I didn't see it at that time, however looking back at photos I can see I was a kind, joyful and beautiful soul. I can see in photos that my smile lit up a room. I had sunshine within me, beaming out.

I can only find twelve poems from my teens, though I am sure I wrote many more. I hope you like those that I could find.

COMING-OF-AGE MEDITATION

*T*his meditation is a wonderful experience you can come back to time and time again.

1. Sit up nice and tall, with a proud chest. Pay attention to where you are connected to the ground or chair.

2. Think back to your teenage years - the first years of high school, sweet sixteen, turning eighteen… Imagine yourself vividly.

> *What are you doing?*
> *What clothes and shoes are you wearing?*
> *Where are you?*
> *Who is with you?*
> *What music are you listening to?*

3. Think of a moment when you felt so excited about something in these special years. Maybe it is something epic like passing your driving test or getting your exam results, or something fun like a sleepover at a friend's house or one of your birthday parties.

4. Vividly seeing your teenage self, now close your eyes and tell them they are awesome, tell them what they need to hear. In this moment, listen to what your teenage you says back to you.

5. Breathing in through the nose and out through your mouth, sighing to release and inhaling to harness the energy and joy of this moment.

YOUR TEENAGER YEARS

*P*oet Prompt:

What did your meditation bring up?

Write down three words to represent your teens.

Jot down any memories and learnings here…

TEARS OF A CLOWN

Born into safety, happiness and love,
To a company of angels as if from above.
Laughing and smiling to keep bad dreams away,
While helping all people to get through the day.

The secret of a clown is to keep control,
Of all emotions, don't let too much show.
The number of these is extremely few,
For I know that for most it's impossible to do.

As with all, deep inside lives a great fear,
Of losing those close, therefore keeping them near
As a comfort, ensuring they never depart,
For even a jester needs a queen of hearts.

Every day for a clown is the same say the crowd.
We can tell by your presence, so confident and loud.
But when the sun sets, bringing the day to an end,
The clown returns home with its shadow as a friend.

Now at the end, as the curtain goes down,
Family and friends of the clown stick around.
We know that life has yet surprises and fun,
And the clown's adventure has not quite begun.

To all other clowns, and you know who you are –
Be aware of your presence, shine out, be a star!
Remember to laugh, and never to frown,
For no one expects tears from a clown.

This poem feels like my most 'famous' poem. It was very well received when I showed my family and when I performed it aloud at a school talent evening. A few audience members even asked me for a copy of it after my performance. The highest praise of all, as far as I am concerned, is that my father kept a copy of it next to his bedside.

Poet Prompt:

Expressing ourselves can be really challenging. Try to express yourself through a poem. Think about a great metaphor for yourself and how you feel about your life. It can be so special to see what comes up.

BEN

Charcoal black,
They stand bright in a coat of pure white snow.
Thick and lovely and so warm.
He lives a life of pure satisfaction.
Content, his eyes hold his gratification.

This one is about Ben the Golden Retriever, our childhood family dog.

Poet Prompt:

Write about your pet. Close your eyes and imagine your favourite moments with your special furry friend. Let the paws patter, the whiskers whisper and the words flow.

YOU

Dancing and laughing and singing
And loving burn in my heart when I see you.

You can say a lot with a few words. This was about a deep feeling of happiness I experienced when seeing someone.

Poet Prompt:

I challenge you to write a one-line poem about anything you like.

LOST THEN FOUND

There was a day when I had a magical dream.

I remember singers and dancers,
And beautiful honest eyes.
Those eyes told me a wonderful story,
That one day we would meet again…
And you would whisper softly to me:
"Jy is bale spesiaal vir my".
We would laugh and smile together,
Instead of wondering, worlds apart.
We would talk one tongue,
And live one language.
We could look upon all the colours of the world,
Bold, bright and beautiful,
As they form a rainbow, the sun would shine beams,
Through all cloud,
Sending hope that one day we will be this dream.
Honest smiles will grow wide,
Reminding me of all good in the world.
Those beautiful, honest eyes will capture
The sunflower's dance.
Their singing will never grow old.

This poem was about a whirlwind friendship... and then my imagination running away with me!

Poet Prompt:

Is there someone who made a lovely impact on your life, that you are no longer in touch with? Write about them. Daydream it all out!

KITE

Love made me fly up high.
I ran and danced in a navy-blue sky.
The glitter stars were sticky and bright,
The planets were round as a triangle is a kite.

It wasn't my fear of falling that gave me reason
To run and launch into maybe.
It was but love that made me dance,
Into a sky of chaos and chance.

Teenage years often bring up our first feelings of young love, lusts and idols. Do you remember your first crush, first hand-hold, or first kiss?

Poet Prompt:

Choose a metaphor for a love you have experienced and make it as bright and wonderful as your memory. Use colours and metaphors to add vibrancy to your words.

COMFORT

Smile at me once and I'll walk away.
Frown at me once and I won't go away.

Poems can be super simple.

Poet Prompt:

Write a poem about opposites.

SECRET

Once a word spoken, once a secret told,
You may take it back, wish you'd better known.
Though now it's free, set to travel the world,
That secret of yours, it's now on its own.

Ah, secrets.

Poet Prompt:

Do you have any secrets? Is there anything no one knows? Perhaps something that only a handful of people know? Write about what it feels like to entrust another person with your secret...

FREEDOM

Today is tomorrow,
Tomorrow, today.
The day is the night,
And the night is the day.
You are not I,
And I am not thee.
Unlike today and tomorrow,
We, like angels, are free.

How free are we? As free as we want to be, or confined by the rules of society?

Poet Prompt:

Have a think about something set in stone, like time, the days of the week, the alphabet perhaps, or roads on a map. Now see what words come to your page when you think about this structure, versus freedom.

A NEW DAY

I will prove you wrong,
And you will regret,
Those negative things
That were once said.

Time will tell the harm you've done,
Daring to take away the laughter and fun.
It is a new day as we keep being told,
So, use it for you and leave me well alone.

I will prove you wrong,
You may learn to regret,
For I choose to forgive,
I never forget.

I pray for bullying to end for everyone. I pray that we can all be ourselves and that no one should feel scared to be at school, at their workplace, on social media, or anywhere.

Poet Prompt:

If you have ever been bullied or not been able to be your full self, write about it here… release it and forgive it.

Likewise, if you may have bullied someone else at any time in your life, here is a chance to forgive yourself, release it and forgive it. It was not your fault. This will take great courage, but it will change your life.

LITTLE LITTLE

Those eyes tell a story from deep in the soul.
Your mood is determined with a blink.
What do you gaze at sweet, little child?
Is it something beyond, beyond?
Those deep blue eyes, what do they tell?
Will it be a story of success?
Your patience, courage, delight,
Will prove to make up for your innocence.

This is a reflective poem, to my inner child.

Poet Prompt:

Who is your inner child? What are they like?

Give them a name (for example, little Jenny) and gently invite them into your mind now, so you can write a poem talking directly to your inner child. This one can be challenging, so if now isn't the moment, come back whenever you wish... no matter what, your inner child loves you very much.

CIRCUS

It feels like there is a circle in my head.
Tigers roaring,
Twirlers dancing,
Musicians playing,
Children singing, laughing,
And clowns,
Oh, the clowns.
Bright, sunny and wonderful.

How active is your mind day to day? Before knowing about anxiety and overwhelm, this is how I described my young mind.

Poet Prompt:

Note down how your mind feels today. What words might you use to represent this in poetry form?

IMPRESSIONS

She knew about all things.
A finger in every pie, so they say.
She worked hard while we grew,
And continued longer than most.
Continuous.

He was bursting with energy,
Combining strength with boyish gaiety.
Providing, leading us out to the world.
Small feet following big feet.
Joyous.

They were my beginning,
Are my now,
And will always be in my heart, my soul and my life.

This one is about my parents. I love them unconditionally.

Poet Prompt:

What do you think of when you close your eyes and imagine your parents/carers/grandparents smiling at you?

POEMS OF MY TWENTIES

*M*y twenties took place during the 2000s. These years were shaped by many different things, including some great pop music! They included the end of my university days in England and Canada before I sprang into the workplace in 2008. There were highs and lows. I made friendships for life, and I also suffered my first major trauma with the death of a very close friend. This occurred the same year I moved from the small island where I had grown up, to the big city of London.

London was brutal. It grabbed me by both hands, lifted me, threw me, bullied me, mugged me, whirled me, and eventually spat me right out in 2020, a decade after I had arrived by bus at Victoria Station, as a young woman ready for an adventure.

My time in London also brought back my passion for music. Singing and reading music again felt magical, and I met so many great people at choirs, chorale services, musicals, and memorable socials with brilliant creatives.

Despite the traumas I endured, I love London and I always look forward to a day trip or a short stay with friends. To me, she is one of the best cities in the world, and although she can be so brutal and so tough, she is also incredibly fragile, awe-inspiring and sacred.

TWENTIES MEDITATION

*T*his meditation is a wonderful experience you can come back to time and time again.

1. Take your mind to your mid-twenties.

2. Focus your mind on the words 'self-love' and 'self-esteem'.

3. Repeat to yourself three times:

> *I am beautiful, I am full of love, I am incredible.*
> *I am beautiful, I am full of love, I am incredible.*
> *I am beautiful, I am full of love, I am incredible.*

4. Smile, close your eyes, and picture yourself in your element.

5. Breathing in through the nose and out your

mouth, sighing to let go of insecurities, and inhaling to empower yourself with the truth – you are beautiful, you are full of love, you are incredible.

Enough said!

Poet Prompt:

If you loved this, then repeat this mantra (or words of your choice) to yourself each morning and night for an extra dose of self-love. No matter what age you are, it can be game-changing to work with a daily mantra.

YOUR TWENTIES

*P*oet Prompt:

What did your meditation bring up?

Write down three words that sum up your twenties.

Jot down any memories and learnings here…

WAKING UP IN NORTH AMERICA

Crisp,
A million tri-pointed
Angels dance in the wind,
Like outstretched hands
Ready to welcome one and all.
The sun, the wind, and the sky all pursue,
And they burn the newcomer's skin.
It is never still, for even under the piles of leaves,
And even for the almighty distance,
The newcomer is at one with the land.
Her love, strength and thrill combine
With precious memory
As
She
Wakes
In
North
America.

I wrote this poem at age nineteen while living in Ottawa, the capital city of Canada. It was a beautiful time. I've presented this as a calligram, in the shape of a strong, Canadian Maple tree.

Poet Prompt:

Write your own calligram, using free handwriting or typing, to show words on the page as an image, helping to tell your story with beautiful visual impact.

MONDAY MOURNING

Waking up and rolling round,
Another night sleeping safe and sound.
Dreaming big while I'm awake,
Come on, hurry, there's a buck to make.

Making it work, gotta pay my rent.
Come on, believe me, every penny's spent.
Life's a breeze when you're lost, I mean found!
Run quick, get on the London underground...

I'm going to Canary Wharf, it's a Monday morning,
It's not my fault that I'm still yawning.
Dragged myself from A to B,
Gonna find a broker to marry me!

Tired head and a foolish heart.
Why is my life always falling apart?
My worn-out soul, it needs saving.
Why am I always misbehaving?

I'm going to Canary Wharf it's a Monday morning.
It's not my fault I'm still yawning.
Dragged myself from A to B,
Can't find a broker to marry me!

Ready and eager and full of hope,
Life's a dream when you don't look too close.
I'm finally seeing some light shining through,
Changing my feelings, no longer so blue.

I'm going to Canary Wharf, it's a Monday morning,
It's not my fault I'm still yawning.
Dragged myself from A to B,
Can't find a broker to marry me!

I'm going to Canary Wharf it's a Monday morning,
It's a brand-new day, the day is dawning.
Got myself from A to B
Don't need a broker to marry me!

This one tells a humorous tale of my Groundhog Day style, repeated existence spent in London, for much of my twenties, wondering if I'd be rescued! The words entered my head on the way into work one morning, along with its very own Country music style tune! Ha-ha, so I can sing this aloud, much to the cringe of those around me! I spent a good while hoping Adele or Ed Sheeran might like to release it as their next single… that never happened!

Poet Prompt:

Can you write a poem to music? Can you invent your own tune to sing your poem along to?

THE CITY

Wondrous skylines and beautiful sunsets,
Living the dream without regrets.
Time is our friend and beauty is our sister,
London is magical with Big Ben in its vista.

Run with me to track and train,
Ride with angels again and again.
Let them rest and create new news,
City's no place for singing the blues.

Instead choose jazz, a chorus or opera,
The notes and the pages are not going to stop her.
Dance with the Gherkin, flirt with the Queen,
Paint your own London, there's so much to be seen.

Wondrous skylines and beautiful sunsets,
Living the dream without regrets.
Time is our friend and youth is our master,
London forever will echo life and laughter.

This one was written before the passing of Her Majesty Queen Elizabeth II. I have always loved the Royal family. I think this is due to spending so much time with my maternal grandmother, who was born in 1927, the year after the Queen. My grandma had a lifelong love of the Queen. I recall that we would always play a game of guessing the colour of the Queen's outfit and hat ahead of royal events. Grandma often got it right!

Poet Prompt:

What city have you been most influenced by? See if you can capture that city in words. Fill this page with words that capture the essence of that city, before shaping them into a poem.

KEEP GOING

Running and running,
Keep up, oh, keep up,
Faster yes.
The day rolls on,
The autumn-covered pavement slips so deep
And vast beneath my little feet.
Keep on, oh, keep on,
You can, yes.
The world is real and true.
You press firmly down with each contented step.

We're all so busy, going about our days with lots to do, however, everything starts with one first step.

Poet Prompt:

Write about where your steps will be taking you this week…

BARBIE DOLLS AND ACTION MAN

See my girls on the top shelf,
And my soldier over there.
See the years go by and the days draw in.
Feel the rain come down,
And the wind push on.
Remember the youth, anticipate the new.
See my girls on the top shelf,
And my soldier over there.
See my family, thrice blessed.

This is written in the voice of a parent talking about their children.

Poet Prompt:

Children capture such joy and innocence. Write about your feelings about the children in your life, perhaps your child, your niece, your nephew, or a friend's child. See what comes up for you as you write.

SUSIE

An artist, with palette in hand, delicately fashioned.
With a face that floats a thousand ships.
A field, a meadow, an orchard full of apples.

NICHOLAS

A brother.
A brave soldier building onward and upward.
Dark eyes and open heart.
An ingenious yet modest conjurer, ever ready.
Eager, honest, impressive. Inspiring.

These were written as birthday card greetings for my sister and brother, for their 18th birthdays. I would have been twenty years old at the time. I love to give a gift of words.

Poet Prompt:

Write some heartfelt words for a family member or friend for their next birthday.

POEMS OF MY THIRTIES

*I*t was during my thirties that I found my voice and became a fully independent adult. I'd spent the previous decades asking others for guidance, for permission, and to essentially make my decisions for me. I have loved reclaiming myself and learning to hear my own voice. Nowadays, I take pleasure in decision-making - I have become a real pro at the decision-making process!

During these years, I also fell head over heels in the most wonderful love. We got married on the happiest of summer days, planting a tree for the Queen's Platinum Jubilee. I battled with my fertility, then found purpose and peace by rehoming a shy, abandoned (yet utterly brilliant) dog.

In my thirties, I began to write poetry even more than ever before, as ideas came to me from all over the place. As you'll see in the next chapter, I began to have some real fun with the words, and not just write when something sad, epic, or deeply emotional had happened. Within the poems of my thirties, I capture joy, love, and celebration for this brilliant life we are so privileged to live.

THIRTIES MEDITATION

*T*his meditation is a wonderful experience you can come back to time and time again.

1. Focus on the number thirty.

2. Let's count down thirty mindful breaths, from thirty, down to one.

Each number lasts for one round of breath:

> *30 (breathe in, then exhale).*
> *29 (breathe in, then exhale).*
> *28 (breathe in, then exhale).*
> *Etc.*

3. If you lose count, simply start again at thirty and enjoy the challenge, and then the amazing calming

of your parasympathetic nervous system that this brings.

4. Close your eyes as you focus solely on your counting of breath.

5. As you settle out of practice, breathe in through the nose and out through your mouth, sighing outwards and making an audible 'ahhhh' sound to really release what needs to go…

YOUR THIRTIES

*P*oet Prompt:

What did your meditation bring up?

Were you able to focus on your counting as you breathed in and out?

Jot down any memories and learnings here...

MY PARROT SOUL

My red, yellow, green,
Sexy, lean,
Squawking machine,
Been flying
Shaking,
Making dreams a reality,
My miscongeniality
Pa pa pa parrot sensuality.
Red
Yellow
Green
So sassy lean.
Red, Yellow, Green
Hold me tight
Bright, light,
Try as I might
What a sight,
Fills up my soul,
Shake my tail-feathered,
Raw, walking, talking, sassy, soul-squawking
Reality

This one is a wacky little song of my best inner qualities - my originality, creativity and silliness - represented by a proud parrot! I wrote this one while on an aeroplane on the way to visit my friends, Alan and Danielle, in Aberdeen.

Poet Prompt:

What are your best inner qualities? Which creature in nature would best represent them for you?

YOGA LOVE & JOY

You
Open
Grow
Adapt

Like you're balanced,
Open as your clarity heightens.
Velvet touch, your love is light,
Eternal sun beams out from within you.

Journey from East to West, you rise, and you set.
Over, under, over, under, with every rise and every fall,
You're more courageous somehow ♡

I believe that Yoga is a song of light. It celebrates the brilliance of the rise of the historic Eastern tradition of Yoga, within modern Western culture. Just as the sun rises in the east and sets in the west.

Poet Prompt:

What lights up your world?

SOLIDARITY FROM THE SKY

They fell from the sky,
As beautiful raindrops
Cascading downwards
As far as the eye can see.
A streamlined symbol of solidarity.
Each separate yet somehow one.

Like a firework
And as impressive.
Like a waterfall
Of canvas and man.

Peace fell from the sky,
As leaves in Autumn.
Warmth on their backs,
Thin air all around.

Each one a person,
One of Earth's creations.
Each one so loved.
Each one a soldier.

I wrote this poem after my husband took part in a military parachute jump into the Ukraine in the autumn of 2020, to show solidarity to the Ukrainian people. I am so proud of him and in awe of what he does in life. He is so full of courage, determination and dedication to his work. He who dares…

Poet Prompt:

Write a poem about something in the news today.

PLATFORM 3

Platform 3 is the gateway for me,
Through repeated small towns to the big city.

Today I wait, I wonder, I stare,
I think, dream, plan, in my mind, I dare
To be a rebel, to go against the grain,
To press my face against the window pane
Of the small station cafe,
The waiting room of nothingness.

To scream, to shout from the top of my lungs
Get out, be free, quit this mirage, this lie.
To encourage a change, a daring new way.
A bright opportunity can start from today.
I try so hard to make everyone else see
That nothing good can come from Platform 3.

In reality, I know it's best not to say a word,
Not to attempt a rebellion or gather the herd.
I stand up and walk away,
Leave the sheep, on the rat race, to their own destiny.
I know for me, this is the right thing to do.
Today, I'll wait on Platform number 2.

This poem came to me while standing on Platform 3 at Colchester train station.

Poet Prompt:

What would you like to shout from the top of your lungs?

TANDEM BICYCLE

Two is company,
It takes two.
You like me, I like you.

Two wee pals,
Best of friends,
Travel adventures, amazing weekends.

We got that bike,
Two seats, one love,
Rode like legends, cool breeze, sunshining above.

"Pain is temporary,
Quitting lasts forever"
Lance says so! Peddle faster we are too slow!

I took the back,
I'm afraid of down hills,
Let's go go go, seeking adventure and thrills.

You're gone now,
So, does that mean it was all a dream?
If a tree falls in the forest and no one hears it,
Does it make a sound?

We rode for hours
Round Stanley Park.
That bike ride happened; it's etched in my heart.

Two is company.
It takes two.
You are always with me; I will always love you.

This song is a remembering of the bike ride I took with my friend in the summer of 2006, in Vancouver. A few years later, she tragically passed away. As no one else was present for our bike ride, I sometimes wonder if it really happened.

Poet Prompt:

Can you recall an event that took place with someone who is no longer here to remember it with you? Write it all down. Cherish it.

JANE

You were there, magnificent.
You were gone, grief.
You are ten years gone - decade decayed.
Your soul, magnificent.

This one was written on the ten-year anniversary of my friend's passing.

Poet Prompt:

If you are grieving, write down the name of your lost love and let your heart pour out onto the page. Don't hold anything back. Remember, grief = love.

MARY

Three Marys, you know what that means!
Crying with laughter, bursting at the seams!
New coat, such long arms.
Velcro shoes, safe from harm.
Corned beef, Jacket potato,
Looking for a hug, you've not far to go.
Watching Hyacinthe, and the dancing.
On the landing, smiling and prancing!
Sitting with Smokey, the best ever cat,
In the flower garden, wearing your Miss Marple hat.
Mary, my grandma, my light, my best friend.
I treasure each moment, each memory you send.
You were kindness, love and community.
You showed me every value I now have within me.
Thank you for joy, for laughter, for your love.
Now you're shining light in heaven above.
You are everything a grandmother could be.
Now I see you are so much more, you're an angel.
You are free.

This one is about my grandmother. To me, she represents all that is beautiful about the world.

Poet Prompt:

Write down ten words that symbolise your grandmother.

WILLIAM

Love me, thrill me, hold me, keep me.
Change me, shape me, give me, seek me.
Build with me, create with me,
Laugh with me, cry with me.
Play with me, run with me,
Dance with me, fly for me.
Fulfil me, make me, win me, wed me.
Monday me, Tuesday me, all through to Sunday me.
Spring me, Summer me, Fall for me, Winter me.
Morning me, day me, dawn me, and night me.

This one is about my gorgeous husband, William. He makes me happier than I knew it was possible to be.

Poet Prompt:

Can you put words to paper to describe your true love?

WILMA

When I think of you
My eyes get wet
With swells of cosy tears.
My heart and body warm up
And I smile.

I thought I couldn't love any more,
Like I'd reached my love capacity.
And then you came into our lives.
I marvel at this love.

You are more brilliant
Than you will ever know.
More kind, graceful
And pure-hearted
Than we could have ever dreamed.

You are joy.

You are curious, clever,
So unique.
Like a tiny lamb when you sleep
Yet like a tiger when awake.

You are the jam in our jam sandwich.

We didn't even realise you were missing,

Before you arrived.
And now I wonder how we survived without you.

Our little, brilliant, beautiful,
Clever girl.

Out gift,
Our jam,
Our pride,
Our bonus love,
Our best friend,
Our Wilma.

This one describes our beautiful dog, Wilma. We rehomed her from the Dog's Trust in 2021. She is a very special creature. What is even more special is that she shares a birthday with my grandma, who passed away the year Wilma was born...

Poet Prompt:

Write a happy poem about your beloved pet. Then read it aloud to your pet! Poetry can be very calming for animals too.

TREE WALK

Do you want a little tree walk?
Do you want a walkie to the field?
I love you so, my Wilmeo, forever more.
You are mummy's little angel, Wilmea Moo
You are my golden star.
Do you want a little tree walk?
Let's go to the field.

Do you ever sing silly songs? I sing this to my dog Wilma to ask her if she would like a walk. There is nothing like watching her leap four feet into the air with joy, gesturing that yes, she would LOVE a walk!

Poet Prompt:

When you connect with animals in the wild or your own family pets, what emotions arise within you? Note these emotions down. Get some colouring pencils to shade colours around the words you have written.

COMPLETE

She ignores me
I don't exist
To her I am nothing

I vanish from her life
Her words, her thoughts, her being.

A whisper
Softly leaves her lips
Who?

I am renewed
No longer an imprisoned failing fiend

Her anguish
Her lament of torment
Her green eyes

My freedom
My chance
My number
I can be whole
Not half anymore

I am for the first time
Complete.

Not every poem is a happy story. This one tells a bittersweet situation and a coming to terms with a new acceptance, which in turn, brings calm of mind, and a huge relief.

Poet Prompt:

What is the biggest worry you have in your head? Write it down. Muddle through it and see if you can find any way to achieve calm and acceptance. Write it all down.

Seeing words written on a page can reveal that sometimes what we think is a real complex dilemma, can be a very manageable challenge to solve. The words might even reveal that there is not actually anything to solve after all. You got this.

LOST FOX

My mother wrote a poem,
It was so good,
It was about a young fox
Who was misunderstood.

It told a lovely story.
It made us smile wide.
The words of the fox were magic to us,
They filled us up with pride!

As the years went by and by,
The poem somehow disappeared.
We searched our papers, texts, emails,
Found nothing, just as we feared.

To this day, we have never found
Those beautiful forgotten words.
They now live within the whispers,
Within the tweeting of the birds.

Perhaps the piece of paper,
Where she first wrote it down.
Might be inside the attic, in a dusty storage box.
Perhaps we will never know what happened
To that precious little fox.

Growing up, I remember my mum wrote a brilliant poem about a fox. It was clever, with great wording and curious just like a real fox.

Poet Prompt:

Have you ever lost anything precious? Note down your faded memory in your journal and write a prayer to honour what has passed before. Read it aloud.

STRONG SWEET SPELLS

They came together on the white isle,
Each from their own unique walk of life.
Open, excited, curious, hopeful, stuck,
Ready to recharge, rest, reset.

They came together,
Sweat, tears, laughs,
Heart opening,
Sharing dreams, revealing fears.

Daily their words made spells,
Transformation, Progress, Energise, Gratitude,
Even Limoncello...

Beautiful women,
All sisters, all mothers,
All daughters of mother earth,
All goddesses of the divine

Reminded to remember why,
All shown lightness, brightness,
Shown how to shine
Under the harvest moonlight.

They came together,
Ebbed, flowed, meandered,
Grew separately,

Yet somehow grew as one.

They came together
As a beautiful tribe,
Armed with strength, guidance, love,
Now knowing they belong.

Worked hard,
Out of their comfort zones,
Physically, spiritually, emotionally,
Energetically, metaphysically.

Sister,
Light up your heart,
Stand your ground.
Know and believe,
What a beautiful human you truly are.
Tell your story,
Be authentically you,
Close your eyes,
Know this sweet truth.

I wrote this while in a taxi to the airport in Autumn 2022, after a really special women's wellness retreat in Ibiza. My brilliant friend, Kelly, told me that when she read it after I left the villa, she burst into tears. I got great feedback from the retreat sisters. They are a beautiful and incredibly special group of ladies.

Poet Prompt:

Write a poem during a taxi ride. Feel the adrenaline and words fly from your mind to your page.

CHRYSALIS

A dark tomb
A sterile state
Nothingness breeds resentfulness
Hope turns to hate
Time ticks it stands still
Still as frozen water droplets
Hanging suspended in mid-air
From a lifeless waterfall

Then without warning
Cracks start forming
Morning dawning
Light shards breaking through
Revealing glimmers of gold
Diamond revelations
Star constellations
An invitation to emerge
To reclaim your birthright
Your destiny
Your starlight
You step into that welcoming light
No longer needing to hold tight
No more
No more
No more

You look ahead
Close your eyes to pray
This my child
This is your birthday.

There sometimes comes a time in life when enough is enough. It could be that something you have done for years no longer fits. You have an amazing opportunity to be re-born. Do you long for re-birth, becoming, newness? Or perhaps you have already experienced a dramatic change in your life that has led you to feel brand new.

Poet Prompt:

Close your eyes and take three soothing breaths. With a hand on your heart, thank the child within you for helping you get to where you are today. Believe and know that you can change your tomorrow.

SPIDER WEBS

Spider webs
Ebbing
Blurring
Tip-toeing
Spreading like webbing
Across the tops
Of the metal posts of the silvery fence
They bind the posts together
Make them one, whole.

Yet we know, just like snow, they will go
With the simple touch of a hand
A wave of a magic wand
Of fingery digits
Hands that fidget
Turning beauty to nothingness
Gone in an instant.

Yet we know, just like snow,
They were there.

On a morning walk with the dog, I spotted glistening spider webs on a fence.

Poet Prompt:

Go for a walk, looking mindfully at everything up close. When you get home write about something you see in nature.

HOLD ON

Hold on,
I got a hold on you
You got a hold on me
We hold ourselves deeply
Embraced
Close face to face
In harmony
Holding strong
Holding on on on on and on
To beautiful blissful love
So in love
We hold on.

This poem celebrates love. The hold is not out of desperation or loneliness. Instead, it is out of choice, purposefully, with pure love.

Poet Prompt:

What is precious to you?

What do you hope you hold onto for the rest of your life?

TEACHER

Hello class.
Thank you all so much,
You are all so smartly dressed,
So on time,
So quiet…
So first class!

Irony… such a powerful cheeky thing. Expectation… who makes the rules?

Poet Prompt:

Note down what an ideal day would be like for you, with nothing going wrong, nothing delayed, and everything in balance and harmony.

HEDGEHOG

Ohhh, you kind soul.
Stopping for me!
Leaving me time to get
From here to there,
To calmly walk without a care,
To get safe inside the hedgerow.
Safely, safely inside the hedgerow.

Aww, wee animals. They can be so vulnerable in our modern world.

Poet Prompt:

Choose a lovely animal, any that takes your fancy, and then write a little poem in the voice of that creature.

LITTLE LAMB

Take your time sweet, little, wondrous creature.
Slowly, surely, springlike
Newness arriving to the morning dew, to daffodils,
Bright yellow smiles along the fencing.

Take your time sweet soul, every moment,
Closer to your entrance,
Your turn, your time to be
Here, to be free, to be
Born.

Our world is so special.

Poet Prompt:

What is your favourite time of the year? Why do you think this is?

Jot it all down… then fill up your page with words that represent this special time for you.

THE GREATEST LOVE STORY

You were two
Two of you
Both a pair
A lovely pair
A happy pair
Not a care
In the world….

You were love
Lovely two
Both together
Sweet forever
Forever sweet
You were a treat
So in love…

We were three
They were two
We were five
Now they are lots
You are two
Two together
You are one…

There are so many different types of love. This one is a sweet, generational song to read aloud with a singsong lilt to your voice. Make of it what you wish.

Poet Prompt:

Thinking about your family and friends. Write a poem about the greatest love story you have ever known.

POEM X

Hello, mother of the universe,
Mother Nature.
Beauty, all that repeats.
Seasons, birthdays, sad days.
Summers, winters, holidays.

Hello, Queen of Beauty,
Empress of Age,
Goddess of Time.
Cycling, ticking,
Ebbing on, on, on, and on,
Metronome of yesterday.

Hello, weather woman,
Wise woman of all earthly swells,
Snowflake, sunbeams, rainfall.
Deserts, seas and forgotten lands.

Hello, divine, true healer and helper.
Universal fixer-upper.
Hello and thank you for giving me life,
For teaching me lessons through joy and strife.

Hello, sister,
Shape-shifter, mystical creature,
All time realist-a.
Hard truths, blunt blues,
Happy endings, come on please.

Hello, rock star,
Beautiful, big all star,
Hipster, music-mixer, truth, tunes, joy, freedom.
Eternally you.

Sometimes you must be your own cheerleader. This poem captured a turning point in my life when I gained huge confidence and self-belief. I felt my ancestors behind me, standing with me and empowering me. I felt sensual. I felt like a goddess.

Poet Prompt:

Conjure in massive self-belief. You are absolutely incredible. You are an amazing person. Write from your soul. Pour your confidence and your love onto the pages. Go, sister. Go, brother. You are awesome.

COOL COURAGE

You are like the breeze.
You fly in and out like a breath.

You left me when I needed you.
Winded. Wounded.

You were there for me when I needed you.
Graceful. Joyful.

You are within us all.
You are with me.
Ubiquitous ambition.
You are beautiful.

Courage is our anchor.

Poet Prompt:

Write about what courage means to you. Choose alliteration, metaphor, and powerful words, to create whatever you wish.

LOST FOR WORDS

You are
Greater
Than words
Will allow.

We can say so much with so few words.

Poet Prompt:

Write a poem using just seven words.

THE LIGHTHOUSE

He is my lighthouse,
Guiding me through the darkest seas.
Waves and surf will not stop me.

Dance in the tide,
Ride the seas of love and connect with oceanic soul.
Guide me through the darkest seas,
Heaven sent to bolster me.

He is my lighthouse,
Guiding me through the darkest seas.
Waves and surf will not stop me.

He is my lighthouse, lighting the way,
Transcending through the mystique of life's tsunami,
To meet navy blue velvet charcoal still waters of home.

The Lighthouse is a love-lilt sea song.

Poet Prompt:

Let's work with metaphors… think of something or someone or somewhere that you love. Now, think of something to represent this - for example, you may think of your best friend, and then select a metaphor of a strikingly beautiful field of wildflowers… or your dad might be represented in metaphor form as a crowd cheering at a football match as a winning goal is scored! Let your imagination run free…

THE VOW

I give myself to you
Wholeheartedly

I give my mind to you
My thoughts
My dreams

I give my eyes to you
My visions
My imagination

I give my lips to you
My kisses
My words

I give my heart to you
My warmth
My unconditional love

I give my body to you
My sensuality
My curiosity

I give my feet to you
My grounding
My home

I give myself to you
Wholeheartedly

The Vow is a gift of eternal and unconditional love. It lightly journeys down the chakras in the body, then grounds us at the feet.

Poet Prompt:

Read this aloud. Who do you think of when you read this? Tell them how you feel.

LIGHT

My heart opens, shooting
Emerald and gold light
Outwards,
Magnetically it flies fast as
Literal light to dispel the
Cracks found in darkness.

I love to work with opposites. Here we have lightness and darkness.

Poet Prompt:

Thinking about opposites, write down a pair of opposite things and see if you can put some words together to paint a colourful picture.

BOOLA AND LABOO

Boola lived amongst stars.
Her father could move mountains.
Her mother could turn her hand to anything.

Boola's Favourite days were those,
She spent with her grandma.
Grandma would knit a web of dreams
And fling Boola through sunshine and clouds
Out into orbit.

The best gift Boola received from Grandma
Was her magical blanket friend, Laboo.
Together Boola and Laboo were invincible.

They kept each other warm.
They made each other laugh.
They wiped each other's tears,
And dabbed each other's scuffed knees.

They played. They made.
They pranced and danced.
They stayed best of friends.

As Boola grew tall,
Laboo seemed to get small.

Boola became stronger
And found she no longer
Needed Laboo to help
Her get through.

Laboo became worn,
Tarnished and torn,
Placed in a draw to rest.

Boola one day looked back to her childhood
With great joy.
Thankful for her adventures amongst stars.
If life got her down,
The thought of Laboo would hold back her frown.
For kindness, was in every starry stitch.

I wrote this one as a children's bedtime story. It stars a young girl called Boola, and her blanket called Laboo. I hope that the words spark the imagination of the child, whilst calming them before sleep. I hope that the story comforts adults and gives a lovely nod to nostalgia, memories of their own childhood, and fondness of yesteryear.

Poet Prompt:

What did you find comforting when you were a child?

What do you find comforts you now?

Write a short story to read to someone at bedtime tonight.

DEAR DAD COLLECTION

The following four songs are a special short collection of poems, entitled 'Dear Dad', written to celebrate Father's Day, 2020.

They comprise the words of thirty anonymous contributors, shaped into something beautiful by Jennifer & William Jones.

They are dedicated to:

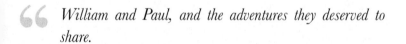

William and Paul, and the adventures they deserved to share.

YOUR OWN

I always thought life was only beautiful and easy,
let me explain why;

You make the best mashed potato!
You always know the answer.
Your patience and quiet words,
Your support means so much.
Your trust in me to do the right thing.
Your strong shoulders
And our adventures to sunshine mountains,
The twinkle in your eye and your cheeky smile.
You weren't there when I was born
Or for my first words,
But you were there for my first day at school.
And you were there when I needed you.
And you treat me like your own.
What I know is you're my dad.
You're like a compass,
Helping me get safely through the journey of life.
Ever grateful for the lesson of porridge versus Frosties,
And your smile of approval, although often rare,
Is worth a king's ransom.
When you put your hand on my head in greeting,
It would give me such comfort, I felt a gentle love.
I need only close my eyes
And think of you to calm my mind.

What makes your father unique? What one thing do you think of when you imagine spending time with your dad?

Poet Prompt:

Write down a list of words that remind you of your dad. Then get your colouring pencils and shade all around the words in colours that match the feeling of those words! What colours do you see?

GOING HAND-IN-HAND

The large hands you once held me with
Now rest comfortably in mine.
When my hands rest within my sons as yours do mine,
I hope he looks back as fondly on his relationship with
His father, as I do with mine.
At eighty-five you are old school
And aware the world has changed,
But you are world-wise of your time.

I truly understood you only when,
I became a dad myself.
Your sacrifices were never seen.
Your pains were never shown.
No asks were too big,
No mischiefs were too bad.
Mum taught me love, but you taught me life.

If I can show my son,
Even half the love you've shown me,
I think I'll be doing just fine.
I miss your dry wit and teasing ways.
Even though you are no longer at home, or at the end of
The phone,
You still listen, encourage and support us in everything
We do.

Do you remember how much you loved football and
Playing the game?
Your grandson plays football and I run his team!
Your granddaughter is off to university this year as a
Talented and beautiful woman.
I never really tell you how much I love you,
So here it is; I really do love you, lots.

Let's think about generations.

Poet Prompt:

Write down as much of your family tree as you can remember… you can always ask another family member for help to fill in the gaps.

It's so good to know where we come from, as our ancestors are alive within us today. They are us.

DID I DO OK?

Dad, did I do ok?

I miss our visits to the pub.
And putting the world to rights.
I miss trying to find the safe place you put your keys.
I miss your running commentary on the TV.
I miss your humour,
But most of all I miss you.
Did I do ok?

I hope you know I made it through.
It hurts you are not here.
I know you had to leave,
But I carry you with me every day.
Did I do ok?

Our last day together just wasn't enough.
I want to ask and show you so much,
If only I had one more day.
Did I do ok?

Dad, you were right,
Things will get better, day by day.

I can see now,
And all I want to say,
Is because of you, I did ok.

It is so natural to feel the need to seek approval. We grow up being told what to do by our parents and teachers without much need to think for ourselves. Entering adulthood can naturally be daunting and a big adjustment.

Poet Prompt:

Do you ever question whether you are doing ok? Write down ten reasons you are doing more than ok… (and you absolutely are).

YOU AND I

Dear Dad, I never got to say goodbye.
And now I don't know how.
I hope I am unlike you,
In the smallest possible number of ways.
When I was a child everyone used to say,
How I looked just like you,
Now that I'm an adult,
I realise how lucky I am to be like you.
You and I, so different and yet so similar,
Both stubborn as marble.
Thank you for inspiring me every day.
Though you are not with me in person,
I know your spirit never left me.
I would love to share one more beer with you,
And have one more outing
To see our football team with the family.
Not a day goes by where I do not think about you.
Even though you passed away so soon,
I still feel incredibly lucky to have you as my dad.
There is no better feeling for me to have,
Then a smile and a hug when I'm back with my dad.

Poet Prompt:

Invite some people in one of your networks to contribute some words on a given topic that you'd like to write about. Wait for the magic to happen. Then make some poems using those words. Honestly, this is such a moving and brilliant thing to do. It becomes even more special when you share the finished poetry with those that contributed.

A MAN AND HIS BORDER COLLIE

SOME DOGS ARE SHY

What does it mean to be shy?
To feel scared of sounds
To be homeward bound

What does it mean to feel scared?
To wish for quiet
To want your bed

What can you do to be brave?
To stand up tall
To speak your truth

What does it mean to be shy?
To feel nervous
To run, to hide

What does it mean to feel scared?
To not go out
To stay in your house

What does it mean to be brave?
To be your true self
To never feel ashamed

What does it mean to be shy?
To be yourself
To be a delight

What does it mean to be all three?
To be shy,
To be scared
And brave all at once?

It means you are thoughtful
It means you are sweet
It means you are the kindest
Doggie we could meet

It means you are light
You are love
You are so strong

It means any lick, any hug
Is deeply fond

It means any step outdoors
Is determined

It means any leap in the air
Is a pure burst of joy, of glee

It means you are honest
You are earnest indeed

Some dogs are shy
Some scared
Some brave
Though often, they are all three
Making the truest companion there ever could be.

Poet Prompt:

Can you delve into why someone feels a particular emotion? Why do they behave in a particular way? Put yourself into the shoes (or paws!) of another being. Strive for deep understanding. Cocoon yourself with compassion.

BEYOND HAPPINESS

*W*ow, what an adventure.

Thank you so much for reading and engaging with the poems and stories within *Poetry Songbook*. I hope that you thoroughly enjoyed journaling and doodling along the way, finding your voice, opening your heart, and unlocking your soul. I hope that your writing is bringing you so much happiness, as well as calm and confidence.

If you haven't already, you can fill this book with your words, wonderings, sketches, doodles, ideas and wishes. If you'd like even more space to write, treat yourself to a blank writing journal. Choose one with a front cover that makes your soul sing.

Remember how special it is to share your words with friends and family. Why not send a poem with the next birthday card you give? This simple act of writing will not only make the recipient feel so special, I guarantee that it will also fill you with joy. Remember, it can be whatever you want it to be. From heartfelt, to hilarious!

Do you know that feeling? Where your head feels clear, you feel energised, optimistic and in your element. You find yourself smiling at strangers and holding doors open for those coming your way, full of gratitude and generally like life is a brilliant gift. This state of mind I like to call our 'happy home reset'. I think, for each of us, there will be that unique something that grounds us and makes us feel at home inside.

As well as writing, it can be so wonderful to remember to engage with your other favourite activities. Cross-train as such! This can leave you even more refreshed to write. I always find a good swim resets me back to my default settings. Growing up, I swam all the time and now, as an adult, I feel that the water connects me back to who I really am.

What is your happy home reset? It could be an activity, or visiting a particular city, town, or special place, perhaps wearing a special outfit, or using a precious pen. It is so valuable to remember what you love. Your favourite places, people and even possessions. Knowing these things helps you to know who you are.

What do you absolutely love?

Poet Prompt:

Think about your favourite activities, places, people, possessions.

Feel free to write yours here, noting when you next plan to engage with each of your happy home resets:

I'd love for you to keep writing and continue to love the feeling of daily creativity, consistent inner calm and an abundance of self-confidence.

If you are keen to develop your poetry writing, you can join my Poetry Club.

You can find me on Instagram @PoetrySongbook

You can also revisit the Poet Prompts within this book anytime you are looking for inspiration.

If you loved the meditations and mindfulness moments, you may wish to join my weekly Yoga Nidra deep relaxation sessions.

You can find out more on Instagram

@heartmindandsoldieryoga

or via my website www.heartmindsoldier.yoga

Huge congratulations to you for completing this poetry adventure.

Remember, you are someone's hero.

Remember, you are wonderful.

I wish you so much happiness, my friend,

With my love,

Jennifer Mary x

BEAUTIFUL THANK YOUS

I am filled with gratitude.

*F*irstly, thank you with all my heart to you, kind reader, for choosing my book. I hope it brings you as much happiness, as it has brought to me.

A huge thank you to my Publisher, Abigail, for her support from day one. This book has been a lifetime wish of mine and Abigail has made my dream come true. Thank you to the whole incredible team at Authors & Co.

Thank you from the bottom of my heart to Ruth, for introducing me to Abigail. This conversation changed my life.

Thank you to my absolutely fabulous mother, Maryanne, and to my wonderful father, Alan. They read brilliant stories to me when I was growing up. They have always encouraged me to read, and to write. They will always be my best friends.

Thank you to my whole family for allowing me to share my true self with you all over the years. To my lovely Uncle Neil, for always bringing such calm, as well as making me laugh with his quick wit.

Thank you so much to Susan and Nicholas, for our childhood games, and for helping me put on 'shows' so we could perform poetry and song! Thank you both for such a joyful and magical childhood. You are incredible people and although we are so far apart across the world, I am so proud of you and your beautiful families. I think of you every single day.

Thank you from deep in my heart, beyond this life, to my bonnie grandmother, Mary, to my brave Grandpa James, to my strong Grandad Leonard, and to my fabulous grandmother, 'Nanny' Violet. You are in my heart. You made our family. You are all deeply cherished. Your words shaped me into who I have become today.

Thank you so much to Angela, Karen, and Kelly, for your recent love, laughs, and companionship. You have kept this military wife afloat!

Thank you to my amazing friends for being there through so many great adventures. Here's to more adventures together.

Thank you to my wonderful in-laws, Leanne and Paul, for welcoming me into their family with open arms, so much fun, and consistent love and kindness.

Thank you to the Military and emergency services everywhere, for helping those in need, and for keeping us all safe.

Thank you to my shy border collie dog-child, Wilma Mary Jones, for teaching me patience and tolerance. Thank you for being the most unique and special soul I have ever encountered on this planet. You are magnificent. Thank you for letting me be your mama.

Finally, thank you to my brilliant husband, my true north, William. Thank you for steadfastly believing in me, for lifting me up both emotionally and literally, and for helping me be the best version of myself. With every word I write, I somehow love you more. You are my why. You are my world. You are my happiness.

Printed in Great Britain
by Amazon

29816065R00129